THEN AND NOW
A Journey With God By Faith

By
AUDREY W. MILLS

Copyright © 2015 by Audrey W. Mills

Then And Now
A Journey With God By Faith
by Audrey W. Mills

Printed in the United States of America.
Edited by Xulon Press

ISBN 9781498427791

All rights reserved solely by the author. The author guarantees all contents are original and do not infringe upon the legal rights of any other person or work. No part of this book may be reproduced in any form without the permission of the author. The views expressed in this book are not necessarily those of the publisher.

Copyright © 1991 by Houghton Mifflin Harcourt Publishing Company. Adapted and reproduced by permission from The American Heritage Dictionary, Second College Edition.

Unless otherwise indicated, Scripture quotations taken from the King James Version (KJV)–*public domain.*

Scripture quotations taken from the The Holy Bible, New International Version (NIV). Copyright © 1973, 1978, 1984, 2011 by Biblica, Inc.™. Used by permission. All rights reserved.

Scripture quotations taken from the New King James Version (NKJV). Copyright © 1982 by Thomas Nelson, Inc. Used by permission. All rights reserved.

www.xulonpress.com

Contents

Acknowledgments vii
Introduction... ix
"Then" In The Beginning............................ 11
"Now"... 19

1. My Faith Journey 21
2. What Is Faith?..................................... 26
3. Sickness and Faith................................ 29
4. He Was There All The Time 35
5. Faith Perseveres, No Matter What................ 37
6. Mustard Seed Faith 40
7. The Offspring Of Faith 43
8. Hearing The Holy Spirit.......................... 47
9. The Amazing Grace of God 49
10. God's Grace Is Sufficient 53
11. The Power of God's Presence 58
12. Man's Promise Keeper........................... 62
13. When Fear Knocks 65
14. When Worry Wages 67
15. When Life Is Broken............................. 70
16. Lessons Learned On My Journey 73
17. Conclusion 75

Acknowledgments

Let me say a word of thanks to:
My husband, Wilbert, who demonstrated love and a caring attitude throughout my sickness. What a gift you are!

My primary physician, neurosurgeon, and cardiologist for your professional advice to my family.

Andrea Mills Hines, a loving daughter whose love left me with the assurance that everything was okay. Proofing and typing my manuscript lifted my burden and provided emotional support as my book went from the rough draft to the publisher.

Ann Dyer, your professionalism helped me stay on the right track, and your encouragement helped me write about my journey.

My granddaughter, Shayla Hines, who was a great encourager, who kept me moving in the right directions to do it right.

My son-in-law, Stevie Hines, whose advice relieved me of many worries.

Lake Taylor Rehabilitation Hospital staff for the excellent therapy and attention given to me. A special thank you to Myrtle Jones, switchboard receptionist, and Chiquilla Moore-McCoy, LPN, for their daily visits to uplift my spirit.

My pastor, Rev. Dr. Geoffrey Guns, and First Lady Rosetta Guns for the wonderful church family you have nurtured. My faith journey would not be complete without Second Calvary Baptist Church. Your kindness, love, and help upon my return to my home church, after my surgery, will always be cherished.

My Sorority Sisters of Iota Omega Chapter of Alpha Kappa Alpha Sorority, Inc. You shadowed me with all kinds of love. You will always have a special place in my heart.

The members of Warren Grove Missionary Baptist Church, Edenton, North Carolina. I shall always cherish how the church planned a worship service especially for me at Lake Taylor Rehabilitation Hospital. Your prayers, individual visits, calls, and monetary gifts exhibited the love of Christ.

My niece, Verna Bowden, and Annie Smith, a former teacher, for your frequent checks on my writing progress.

The Interdenominational Ministers' Wives and Ministers' Widows Alliance of Tidewater for your loving spirit during my recovery.

To my readers:

I pray that my book will provide a vision of God's grace as you journey through life by faith.

Introduction
Tell About It

I want to tell the world about having faith in the Lord, specifically, about my faith in the Lord. Why? Because He promised that if I tell the world about Him, He will tell the Father about me! When God has done something for you, don't be a silent disciple. Witness boldly to others about your faith and God's grace.

I wrote this book because I wanted others to find strength in dealing with crises in their lives due to sickness. This book will help you discover the benefits you can receive when you put your faith in God and discover His amazing grace.

This book will help you stay steadfast in faith, whatever the situation is. That's why we celebrate Jesus' last words on the cross, "... It is finished!" (John 19:30). Jesus finished his task with these three words. We are redeemed from the curse because Jesus has already paid the price for us of sickness, poverty, and emotional problems. You will learn to stop doubting God because God can turn the curse into a blessing.

For anyone suffering in body or soul, this book of reflections offers not only enduring insights into the meaning and significance of suffering, but a quiet strength that inspires us to live more fully and with more purpose despite the suffering.

God's plan for our lives isn't generally like a vacation. He takes us through valleys and stretches us beyond our comfort zones. My experience with God's guidance has been one in which the beauty of His choices in leading me through difficult places allowed me to experience the depths of His wisdom and love. God didn't say it would be easy, but He promised His Spirit would be there when we needed Him even though it sometimes feels like you're alone on your journey.

The theme of the book is to put faith into action and expect God's blessings and strength to help you rise above any circumstance.

Each chapter gives you insight or help in building your faith experiences by the grace of God during your trials in life. You can do extraordinary things when you are armed with faith.

Scripture passages and verses are an integral part of each chapter in this book to support and amplify the textual comments.

"Then" – In The Beginning

In 1978, God called my husband, Reverend Wilbert Mills, Sr., to pastor Warren Grove Missionary Baptist Church in Edenton, North Carolina. Warren Grove is seventy-two miles one way from our home in Virginia Beach, Virginia. As a pastor's wife, I accepted the call along with my husband. For thirty–three years, we worked together for the cause of Christ.

Throughout the years, God blessed both of us with good health and stamina. However, in 2009, I began to complain about stiffness in my left leg and lack of balance when walking. Ninety-nine percent of the time, when we arrived at the church, I had to stand for a few minutes when I got out of the car before I could take the first step.

I compensated for my problems because every day was not the same. In spite of what was going on with my body, God allowed me to be successful as I helped my husband develop ministries and initiatives. The visions and programs that were established by God Almighty were successful because God knew what was needed, and He blessed us to lead under His directions.

God has always instilled in my heart that a life lived for others is a life worthwhile. God allowed me to develop and initiate faith-based programs for the church and the community during my husband's pastorate. The following faith-based programs were organized and directed by me as First Lady:

1. Reorganization of the Deaconess Ministry and development of a Deaconess Handbook.
2. Development and organization of the Stewardship Enlistment Ministry with emphasis on tithing.
3. Development and organization of a Scholarship Ministry.
4. Organization and direction of the Christian Education Ministry.
5. Development of an incentive program to uplift all students' achievement in school.
6. Development and organization of the College Graduate/College Student Reunion. This event brought together all college graduates and college students of the church for the cause of secular and Christian education.
7. Development and organization of a Church-Wide Institute Program. This initiative invited churches and the community to participate in workshops

for all ages. Appropriate topics were selected for each age group based on issues of today.

God also focused my attention to develop and organize a community faith-based program in 2000-2004 for students in grades three, four, and five throughout the Edenton-Chowan Schools. The acceleration program was held on Saturdays. The main focus was to provide direct instruction to those students who scored the lowest on the reading and math sections of the North Carolina State Standards Tests. Certified teachers in the community, in the church, and from Norfolk and Chesapeake, Virginia volunteered to teach. Teachers selected their subject preference and grade level. Each teacher had a teacher's assistant.

Lesson plans were provided for the teachers in advance along with appropriate follow-up activities. However, teachers had the autonomy to write their own lesson plans. At the end of each session, teachers administered a mastery test of six items to tap into what was taught during the sessions. Bus transportation was provided for the students; however, parents also assisted by bringing their children to the sessions and assisted during the snack period. Sessions were held at Warren Grove Missionary Baptist Church and at D.F. Walker Elementary School from nine a.m. to one p.m. The principal and the instructional specialist from the Superintendent's office provided material and resources. This initiative resulted in improved test scores for the students in the Edenton-Chowan Schools.

In 2005 through 2009, emphasis was placed on parent education via parent seminars held for parents in Edenton. Parents were involved in workshops dealing with helping their children at home with homework, discipline, and the importance of parental involvement with the school. Emphasis was also placed on money management and other home-related problems.

When we work for the Master, things happen. We have to make the effort and then trust God to bless our work until it succeeds.

My productive life continued because God was in charge, and I really wasn't concentrating on anything but serving others through the church and the community. However, life changed when my husband and I went on a cruise to Venice, Italy and Athens, Greece with my daughter and son-in-law and friends in celebration of my granddaughter's graduation from Indiana University. The cruise was from May twenty-eighth, 2010 through June seventh, 2010. I survived and coped with the long walks, tours, and the excitement of having a good time.

Traveling back to the States was when I encountered problems. The flight from Italy to Paris was fun and enjoyable. However, from Paris to Dulles International Airport in Northern Virginia was a nightmare. Everyone was complaining about the freezing temperature on the plane. It was a twelve-hour flight from Paris to Dulles International Airport. Despite my being covered with a blanket and wearing a jacket, I felt little comfort.

As we traveled from Dulles International Airport to Silver Spring, Maryland, I experienced severe stiffness in my legs. When we arrived at my daughter's home in Silver Spring, I was unable to navigate the steps to the front door and fell to the ground as I attempted to use the steps.

Because of my condition, Wilbert and I left Silver Spring, Maryland around nine-thirty p.m. and arrived home at one-thirty a.m. on June eighth, 2010. After arriving home, I received little to no sleep. I had severe pains in my neck, which lasted for three weeks.

On July third, 2010, I went to the Emergency Room. The doctor on duty gave me a pill for pain, which only gave relief for one day.

The next day, July fourth, 2010, I returned to the Emergency Room. The doctor on duty listened to my problem and immediately sent me for an x-ray of my neck. The x-rays showed arthritis on my spine. He gave me a prescription to take for seven days.

The medication relieved the pain, but it was a steroid. The doctor recommended an MRI and referred me to my rheumatologist and neurologist as a follow-up. My rheumatologist did not recommend an MRI. However, my neurologist followed up with the MRI. The results of the MRI showed a minute spot on my spine in the neck area which was identified as a benign tumor. Thank God it was not malignant. My primary physician recommended a neurosurgeon. My conference with the neurosurgeon consisted of him sharing with me the MRI films and his recommendations to remove the tumor. He stated, "If you do not have the surgery, you will be paralyzed for the rest of your life or be in a wheelchair for the rest of your life."

On September seventh, 2010, the cervical spine surgery was performed. I remembered little after the surgery. I was told that I developed shingles after the surgery, had an elevation of blood pressure, and high sugar readings. It is amazing how God protects us from seen and unseen danger. Before the surgery, the prayers of my husband and family gave me peace and comfort.

As I tried to recover at home, the nurses around the clock prayed for me daily. My husband and daughter were also prayer warriors. In my heart, I expressed to God how thankful I was for blessing and enriching my life from the prayers of others.

As I prayed to God, I thanked Him for giving me a peaceful feeling when I prayed. I was thankful for the many wonderful blessings He sent me each day. My theme song was *One Day At A Time* with my favorite phrase, "Yesterday's gone, sweet Jesus, and tomorrow may never be mine."[1] Therefore, I thanked God for His new mercies every day.

Early in the mornings as I lay in my bed at home, I rejoiced over the rising of the sun and its beauty. God wants us to be like the rising of the sun, filled with the rays of heaven. It was my time to thank God for the new mercies of the day and to rejoice and beam over the gladness of the Spirit of the Almighty.

Each day, I believed that my change was coming. I believed that all things are possible with God and that possibility is the greatest thing of a person's life. I prayed every day for God's divine healing, but I realized that I had to be patient and wait on God's time. God's divine purpose is to change our weaknesses into mighty strength and faith. This strength and faith had to be built on a foundation, which is the Word of God.

I confessed that I needed to be true to God. Reading a daily devotional doesn't take the place of the Word from the Bible. The foundation of all things is the Word.

I was grateful to God because He listened with great understanding to my hopes and needs. In my prayers, I let God know that He was at my side always and that He has a real and loving concern for me. I was determined that my sickness would not rob me of the potential of the future. When you wait in faith and patience without fretting and without questioning God's wisdom, life affords you an opportunity to grow in faith and wisdom. When you put your faith in God and trust Him, He will let you know that He is with you when you hurt.

The love and resiliency from my family played an important part in my life. My husband, daughter, granddaughter, and son-in-law managed to get through the labor pains without a shadow of a doubt as they cared for me. They managed to get through the experience by standing on the shoulders of God. My husband, Wilbert, confessed that he was able to take care of me by drawing close to God and leaning on God's strength. All of his daily activities were solely concentrated on me and my welfare. His prayers would always refer to Psalm 30:5 (NKJV) which reads "... Weeping may endure for a night, But joy comes in the morning." We both believed that the sorrow we felt together would lead to a better tomorrow. There is the promise of future joy amid our tears as we lean upon the Lord.

"NOW"

My Faith Journey

"Now" is the time for me to reflect more on the goodness of God and how He guided me on a faith journey since 2010. Now is my time to praise God for a better understanding of my spiritual growth.

As I journeyed with God by faith, there was not a designated route or predetermined destination. Rather, my journey was more spiritual because it allowed me to broaden my image of God about "becoming rather than being", about asking questions, about always moving forward toward the heart of God.

During my faith journey, my desire was to advance in my faith by facing and overcoming obstacles and difficulties and not to give up during my struggle with pain. My faith journey was an opportunity to understand the nature of God and how His almighty power took care of what I needed. He used my suffering to bring me to a new commitment when He answered my prayers.

The Bible was my guide and food for the journey. My prayer life was restored because sometimes I lacked spending proper time with God at the beginning of the day. Once my prayer life was restored, my prayer time was a deep and personal conversation with God. My prayer time on a daily basis was a time to acknowledge God's presence in and around me. As my faith grew, my trust in God carried me through all my human experiences.

As I traveled on my journey, I found joy on the freeway of faith. However, the thief will try to take you down the wrong path so you will detour off the freeway of faith. When you start complaining, worrying, or trying to fix the situation yourself, these detours will put up a roadblock.

In order to get back on the right road, you must keep on believing the promises of God by faith and wait on God to receive your blessing.

Remember that as we journey with God by faith, adversity may show up, but we must praise God anyway. For we walk by faith and not by sight. By faith, we can walk securely, one day at a time. That day is today. In Matthew 6:34 (NIV), we read, "Therefore do not worry about tomorrow, for tomorrow will worry about itself. Each day has enough trouble of its own." Even when we are obedient to the Lord, the skies of adversity may not always clear immediately. Circumstances may get worse before they improve. But praise God, His grace will sustain us, and the storm will pass. Pain will either turn us against God or draw us to Him.

Since my operation, I have witnessed the new year of 2011, 2012, 2013, 2014, and 2015. In my mind, I reflected on who took care of me as each year was ushered in. Deuteronomy 11:12 (NKJV) reads, ". . . The eyes of the Lord your God are always on it, from the beginning of the year to the very end of the year." My faith allowed me to confess that I would not fear the future because of what happened to me September seventh, 2010. Because of my faith, I will not be chained to the past because I can move ahead when I focus on God.

The benign tumor, minute and cushioned on my spine, dictated attention, but God, all powerful, had the last move. God orchestrated a melody of faith so I could celebrate and witness His love, power, and joy. A drumbeat grappled a melody on my heart to linger on.

The "what" of my future is determined by the "who" of my eternity. My journey allowed me to refresh my stale faith. My faith became alive on my journey.

Now I'm taking the responsibility to improve my walk by faith. Walking by faith with God teaches us to listen, to hear His voice. God has all power and He knows what we need. When we accept Jesus Christ as our personal Savior, the Holy Spirit comes into our lives and seals us as children of God. From this amazing experience, we are meant to grow in our walk with God. We get to know God in a personal way and discover His purpose for our lives. It is important that we learn to listen to and obey Him, experience His presence, power, and wisdom, and understand what it means to live a Christian life. Those who are not walking in the spirit and trusting God are not advancing in their faith or being used by God for His glory.

My journey taught me to face adversity and trials. God designs trials to achieve His purpose. God knows exactly how to strengthen us spiritually in proportion to our faith. We must understand the nature of God. God the Father wants us to know Him better. Therefore, we must comprehend that He is omnipotent, omnipresent, and omniscient as well as holy, righteous, merciful, and kind. As I began to understand the totality of the God who reveals Himself through His creation and Word, my faith began to grow.

Christian faith is not a method for getting God to do what you want Him to do. It is a life of dependence on Jesus, learning to let Him do what he wants to do through you.

As I journeyed by faith, I depended upon God's mercy, forgiveness, and undeserved kindness. I learned to depend on Him when things are good and when they are not good. It means we trust even when we don't understand.

As Christians, we do not walk by what we see, but by faith. We never walk alone. Where would I be today without God's presence during the frightening descents and sharp curves I experienced on my journey? There have been days of great sadness, pain, and fear, but I knew

God was with me. The side effects from certain medications were painful to my body, but God heard my prayers, and He surrounded me with His presence and power.

My journey is a journey of gratitude. I thank God for His steadfast presence in sorrow, despair, and fear.

What Is Faith?

Hebrews 11:1 describes faith as "... the substance of things hoped for, the evidence of things not seen." This tells us that faith is a conviction that we have regarding something that allows us to be able to act on it as if it were assumed to have happened. If you have true Christian faith, you do not need to search for the evidence; you already possess it. Real faith is any promise made by God. This is the evidence. What God promises, He will perform. Real faith comes from the Spirit of God. It is the fruit of the Holy Spirit. No one can have it or even be a true Christian without God's Spirit.

The Word says in Hebrews 12:2 that Jesus is "the author and finisher of our faith. . . ." Jesus is not only the author but the originator of faith. He is the one who perfects it in us. Faith is not something we do or a presence of mind that you develop; it is a gift from God that we receive from the Word of God.

In Smith Wigglesworth's book on Faith, he states, "that the foundation of faith is the Word—and today we need to have our faith built upon the Rock. If you are on the Rock, no powers can move you. If you build on anything else—such as, sentimentality, imagination, any feelings, or any special joy—but the Word of God, it will mean nothing without the foundation."[2] Faith has the power to make you what God wants you to be; only you must be ready to step into the plan and believe His Word. Wigglesworth also states "we should read the Word through, write it down, pray it in, work it out, and pass it on."[3]

Steadfast faith spreads strong in a whirlwind, soars high with the identity of an eagle bird flying in the wind, and grows roots downward into the past, nourished by the redeeming love of God. Faith is not something we only exercise during life's moments of crisis. It is not just something to consider when things aren't going well. It is full time. We must lean on it everyday. This Christian walk is not easy; therefore, we must walk by faith, not by sight.

During my faith journey, I witnessed that the greatest faith of all is when you live day-by-day trusting God. I have put my trust in God so much that the problems I encountered during my recovery have been an opportunity to see God's work in my life. I trust God so much that I look at all my problems as being an opportunity to draw closer to God because of His amazing grace. Many days after praying and reading the Word of God, my pains disappeared and I found comfort in the Word. In Hebrews 4:12 (NKJV), we read, "For the word of God is living and powerful, and sharper than any two-edged sword, piercing even to the division of soul and spirit, and of joints and marrow, and is a discerner of the thoughts and intents of the heart."

God wants to purify our minds until we can bear all things by faith.

Sickness and Faith

Dealing with my sickness was particularly difficult. I was seventy-eight years old when it was discovered that I had a minute benign tumor on my spine in the neck area. I thought that after surgery and therapy, I would be up and well. I had hope in my heart where faith should have been. Now I know that hope will not produce the thing desired because hope is really a goal setter. The healing prayers of my husband, family, and ministers of the Tidewater Metro Baptist Ministers' Conference of Virginia were greatly appreciated.

The issue of sickness was a top priority on my journey. The key is remembering that God's ways are higher than our ways. When we are suffering with a sickness, disease, or injury, usually the focus is on our own suffering. In the midst of a trial of sickness, it is very difficult to focus on what good God might bring about as a result. God can bring about good from any situation. My sickness allowed me to grow closer to God, to trust Him more, and to learn how to value life. We do not have power of ourselves. Everything we have has come from the goodness of God. God gave us His only begotten son, Jesus. He died for us in spite of many deserting Him. We cannot save ourselves, and we cannot heal ourselves. Therefore, true faith is giving ourselves completely to Jesus no matter what happens. Trusting Him totally with our lives knowing He is good and will do what is best for us is faith.

This trusting faith in Jesus allows us to magnify God in our lives for all the world to see. God's character and sovereignty direct human drama when Faith and Sickness dialogue.

The antagonistic behavior of Sickness allows her to travel and collaborate with her two companions, Suffering and Death. When Sickness speaks, she may say, "You have an ailment that no one can cure, therefore, I will be with you for a lifetime."

Faith gawks at Sickness and remarks with a tone louder than a thunderstorm or earthquake, "Your dominating presence influences and disrupts peoples' lives. The speed with which you travel varies and your advent appears either subtle or tumultuous."

Sickness responds to Faith by interrupting, "I do not discriminate, and I am no respecter of persons."

Faith retorts, "You may not be a respecter of persons and do not discriminate, but you do not come by invitation.

One of the reasons you show up is when a person neglects one's self."

Faith challenges Sickness by acknowledging, "I can overcome you. Don't be overwhelmed. Accept it. Everything in life that we accept undergoes a change. Therefore, let suffering and sickness become love when we seek God's will for our lives and accept His sovereign right to define our suffering and healing."

Because God is a sovereign God, He knows the end results and will take care of every situation. However, we should not let our "faith tank" get low or on empty because faith is supposed to grow. When my sickness fell upon me, I cried out, "Why is this happening to me?" Never did I dream of sharing a faith story in writing. God guided me toward a higher goal that I would not have moved toward otherwise. Life difficulties can be a mechanism for growth when we allow God to have the first place in our lives. God assures us that if we sit at the feet of Jesus, our faith will grow. You don't have to squeeze in more religious activities, buy more religious books, or restart your daily devotions. Just have an encounter with the one whom your faith depends from start to finish. Remember, keep your eyes on Jesus. Mary did when she sat at His feet (Luke 10:38-42).

Jesus was a great physician, a healer whose time was consumed with people who were sick, blind, deaf, leprous, paralyzed, or mentally ill. What cured these people was their faith in Jesus. That's all He asks of us today as well.

In the Book of Job, we are told, "Man who is born of woman is of a few days, and full of trouble" (14:1). All of us have sensed that life seems short, and most of us have had plenty of troubles. We are living in a world of trouble. This world is filled with heartaches and suffering of all kinds. No one is immune from troubles. The rich suffer as well as the poor. The proud suffer and so do the humble. The sinners suffer and so do the saints. Wherever one turns, he finds suffering and sorrow and headaches. There's suffering from sickness, suffering from infirmities of advancing age, suffering from disease, suffering from poverty, suffering from mental anguish, and on and on one could go.

Job's story illustrates how we should respond and understand some of the deep mysteries of life. It is addressed to our faith in God and His ways and how we should trust God when we cannot understand Him. Job was a godly man reduced from wealth and influence to material poverty and physical suffering. His wealth was in flocks and herds, and he was a patriarch to his family.

Job knew God. His faith in God was the framework for the story, which unfolds in the book of Job. Job's success was not just measured by his financial prosperity, but also by his integrity and his faith. He should be applauded for he did not only provide materially for his children, but he also provided spiritually for them by encouraging them in their relationships with God (Job 1:4). Job was a godly man.

Job's account in the scripture is to help Christians trust God patiently as they go through discouraging and traumatic experiences, waiting on God's time line to resolve their problems. Not everything in this life seems fair and equitable.

Job's three friends, Eliphaz, Zophar, and Bildad, came to mourn and to comfort him when he lost everything—his children, property, and possessions—all in one day. His friends did not comfort him, but accused Job of committing sin and claimed God was punishing him. In spite of this, Job did not lose faith in God. He knew whom his Redeemer was and that He was a living Savior. His friends said Job was suffering, and God was punishing him for some secret sin that Job was hiding. Job denied this.[4]

Job had another friend, named Elihu, who held Job up in high esteem. God gave Elihu insight into the true nature of Job's suffering and the suffering of mankind (Job 32:6-8). Elihu knew he got his understanding from the Spirit of God. In the end, Job was healed and blessed twice as much after his trial.[5]

Job's experience teaches us that we may never know the specific reason for suffering, but we must trust in our sovereign, holy, righteous God. Since God's ways are perfect, we can trust that whatever He does and whatever He allows is also perfect. We can't expect to understand God's mind perfectly, as He reminds us, "'For My thoughts are not your thoughts, Nor are your ways My ways,' says the Lord. 'For as the heavens are higher than the earth, So are My ways higher than your ways, And My thoughts than your thoughts'" (Isaiah 55:8-9 NKJV).

I can boldly witness to the love of God and faith in Christ as I endured my sickness in spite of my pains. I refused to be imprisoned with a "give up" attitude. My faith keeps me strong in spite of my weak moments. There is no greater witness to the love of God and faith in Christ than sickness endured with faith and love. I learned to bear my infirmities with virtue, with courage, with patience, with faith and hope, and with gladness and joy.

He Was There All The Time

One year after my September seventh, 2010 operation, my husband and I had a divine visit from the Holy Spirit. As we awakened at six a.m., the Spirit led me to move my body to the foot of the bed to allow my right arm to be free. This made it easy for my husband to lay his hand on the area where I was experiencing pain. He prayed a prayer of healing and asked God to anoint his prayer. In the midst of his prayer, I called out to God and confessed that we both should pray together daily and let God take first place in our lives.

I began to stretch my arm and right hand. My walk was balanced and upright. Praises from our lips to God were Hallelujah praises. We cried together and confessed before God about forgiving us for taking His blessings for granted. Waking up in the morning and not praising God in prayer together should have been a daily ritual. We called our daughter to tell her about the blessing, and she told us that she was in her car in the parking lot at her job crying. She said her tears were of joy, but she had not known why. The Holy Spirit's visitation took place in Virginia and Silver Spring, Maryland at the same time.

Faith Perseveres – No Matter What

November of 2011, I had a set back when I took a prescribed medication for my blood pressure and fluid in my feet and ankles. The side effect from the medication caused muscle cramps in my legs and body, which made it difficult for me to walk. I began to cry out, "Why is this happening?" I was doing so well and had just celebrated one-year recovery from my surgery. My thoughts led me to reflect on my faith journey. Did I really believe what I said I believe? Was my faith just a mental agreement that God's Word is true, or was I willing to walk by faith?

In the midst of my negativity, God provided me with a revelation to know that help was on the horizon. It was in God's power to connect me with a cardiology doctor who believed in prayer and who acknowledged that what he did to help patients was God. He understood he was only an instrument used by God.

On June twenty-sixth, 2012, my cardiologist lifted my spirits and my husband's spirits by leading us in prayer and by making changes in my medication regiment and diet. He worked with the odds as I described my side effects after each change of medication. He did not quit or lose patience with me. We both focused on the person of Jesus Christ. My faith allowed me to fix my eyes on Jesus, "... the author and finisher of our faith; who for the joy that was set before him endured the cross, despising its shame, and is set down at the right hand of the throne of God" (Hebrews 12:2). "Consider Him who endured such opposition from sinful men, so that we will not grow weary and lose heart" (Hebrews 12:3 NIV).

Our faith should persevere because Jesus is the one who started our faith by dying on the cross for us. He's also the one who stays with us in the faith, boosting us up in His spirit when we struggle. When I was tempted to quit and feel sorry for myself, I fixed my eyes on Jesus because He is faithful and He promises to reward us in the end.

I learned that real faith perseveres, no matter what. Medication after medication that did not agree with me was a trial I was facing that threatened to discourage me. My prayer to God was to help me stand, not fall; to lift me up, not let me down.

Throughout my journey, Jesus stood with me and would not let me fold up. I shall always remember how Jesus stood alone, stayed courageous, and went all the way to the cross for me. When we persevere through storms and have faith in Christ, we can say with Paul,

I have fought the good fight, I have finished the race, I have kept the faith. Now there is in store for me the crown of righteousness, which the Lord, the righteous Judge, will award to me on that day—and not only to me, but also to all who have longed for his appearing. (2 Timothy 4: 7-8 NIV)

Whenever a checkmate in life strikes, praise God—no matter what. We must measure our faith by our ability to praise God in spite of suffering. Raging storms in life strike bolts of lightning but are defeated when faith perseveres in spite of threats and danger. Instead of waiting for raging storms in life to pass, persevering faith will help you learn to work in the rain. Faith takes the wings of a dove to survive the tempest shock.

Ephesians 1:13-14 (NIV) assures us, as Christians, that we can be confident, that we will persevere because God has given His Holy Spirit to us as a promise that we will succeed.

I thank God for His strength and power as I persevered and endured during my darkest moments. When we transfer our attention on the mighty strength and power of God, we can persevere—no matter what.

Mustard Seed Faith

Jesus talked to His disciples about their faith. In Luke 17:6 (NKJV), Jesus says, "... If you have faith as a mustard seed, you can say to this mulberry tree, 'Be pulled up by the roots and be planted in the sea', and it would obey you." Jesus is speaking figuratively about the incalculable power of God when unleashed in the lives of those with true faith. The key to understanding the passage is the nature of those with true faith, which is a gift from God.

Many years ago as a young Christian, I had heard and read about the mustard seed faith but didn't know about its significance. I didn't realize that God wants us to know that a tiny beginning or substance expands when it comes from Him. As I grew in my Christian faith through the knowledge of God's Word, my mustard seed faith grew and gave me access to God, as well as protection and victory over the difficulties of life. During my daily devotion with God, I experienced a special anointing and a strong feeling in my right hand. My eyes would always look up high to the ceiling of my room, and the blessing of God's presence could be felt. Spending time with God in this manner was a daily ritual for me.

When I became First Lady at Warren Grove Missionary Baptist Church, one of our parishioners became ill and was rushed to the hospital. Her family summoned my husband and me to the hospital. They told us that their loved one was extremely ill and her system had shut down. The Holy Spirit directed me to go into her room alone and lay hands on her as I prayed a silent prayer for her. Her body began to move, and her movement let me know that she could hear the prayer. This parishioner was healed on God's timetable, as God took her through many stages of healing and recovery. Today, she gives her testimony everywhere she goes.

God gives us the measure of faith the size of a mustard seed, and we can use it when we are praying for others or ourselves. Our minds should be focused completely on God because He gave Jesus up for us, and by His stripes and the cross we must look to the power of the Holy Spirit.

On another occasion, a parishioner who suffered from kidney stones passed six kidney stones two hours after I laid my right hand on her stomach and prayed a prayer that shook my body as well as the parishioner's body.

When you look at your tiny mustard seed faith and see Jesus and the power of the Holy Spirit working in your life, you must act on this faith and move any mountain standing in your way.

Today, I'm experiencing a life of faith. I have stopped saying, "I can't" but have started believing that God can! I'm still dealing with certain limitations that go on in my body, but I trust God anyway. When we have mustard seed size faith, we must focus completely on God. My right hand was used by the faith that others would be healed and find comfort. However, after my operation and due to neuropathy, my right thumb, wrist, and arm can be painful sometimes. I believe that the measure of faith that God has given me has stabilized my life in spite of everything.

My faith, not feelings or circumstances, make my life stable. Pain will either turn us against God or draw us to Him. God's blessings will come in His perfect timing, and you have to have the mind of God. We waiver when we focus on our difficulty, pain, or hardship. I have learned not to listen to pity. Daniel survived in the lion's den and went to sleep because he obeyed God. I have learned that when I focus on the hardship, I get more difficulty. When I focus completely on God with my mustard seed size faith, great things get done. Remember, faith is a gift from God. The power of faith reflects the omnipotent nature of God who bestows faith.

The Offspring of Faith

Jesus is the Offspring of Faith. The faith that we have should be placed in Christ in order to have a sure thing. God sent His son Jesus to be our Savior and Messiah--God in flesh to be our Lord, the ruler of our thoughts and mind. We are to know God's ways through Jesus Christ. God forgives our transgressions through Jesus Christ. We cannot produce fruit if we do not know Jesus Christ, nor can we please God. We should allow the Holy Spirit to have power in our lives. The more we submit to the Holy Spirit, the more fruit we will have in our lives.

Sometimes we think that the fruit in our lives are integrity, the accomplishments, the achievements, and the positive impact we have on the world and on people. God teaches us in His Word—the Bible—that no human being can do good works, only God can. Our minds can deceive us to believe that our good works are what God is looking for and that our lives are okay when we try to do good and accomplish good things in this life that are appreciated by other people. Sometimes we might even believe that God appreciates them, and these works satisfy our own desires to be a good person and make us and other people feel good.

But God wants us to repent and change our whole way of thinking and make a turn away from everything that prevents us from seeing God and obeying Him. The fruit God desires is the knowledge of Jesus Christ, who is the wisdom of God. This knowledge is obtained when we establish a relationship with Jesus and know what He has done for us. When you study and learn about His story as your Savior, how He died to be your Savior, and rose to be your friend and companion, this is the knowledge God wants you to obtain.

Every day, I took a step of faith on God's shoulders because I knew He would carry me across the obstacles of life. Many days as I endured the nerve damage in my right arm, thumb, and wrist, due to neuropathy, I asked, "Lord, how long can I endure the pain?" The uncertainty that I experienced in my daily walk led me to identify my faith and walk with my Savior.

Many days, I would get caught up in special TV shows and programs and, unfortunately, they took priority of my day. I robbed God of many opportunities to meditate, fellowship, and commune together in prayer. Therefore, I had to make a change from a behavior that inadvertently morphed a period of entertainment and TV commercials that promoted medications that promised to correct pain and physical conditions. These shows polarized my attention and elevated false hope.

On Saturday night, June twenty-fourth, 2014, God provided comfort and peace to my aching pain. During the day, I had been reflecting on Psalm 23:4 (NIV), "Even though I walk through the valley of the shadow of death, I will fear no evil, for you are with me; your rod and your staff, they comfort me." Here, God demonstrates love for His children throughout the bad times. The comfort and knowledge received from Psalm 23:4 flooded my mind with a sea of God's amazing grace which allowed me to fade off to sleep with joy.

My experiences on my journey taught me how to comfort others in their suffering because God had comforted me. Comfort involves encouraging and strengthening the afflicted. I provided comfort to others by witnessing to them my own troubles and how God helped me in them. Christian comforting should not make you uncomfortable. In this world, we need to know more about the power of God through His Son, Jesus, the Offspring of Faith.

Christ knows firsthand what we suffer when our bodies and souls are ill. He offered up His suffering so the whole world might be healed. If we have faith, God will help us when we suffer and will help us find ways to reduce the suffering. He will lead us to find strength to endure when suffering cannot be avoided. As believers, we must have the assurance that we have divine assistance to face the challenges of life. Jesus Christ, the Offspring of Faith, is our "Deliverer".

Hearing the Holy Spirit

On September twenty-fourth, 2012 at eight-fifty a.m., I had just completed an exercise session at the Lifestyle Fitness Center located at Chesapeake Regional Medical Center in Chesapeake, Virginia. My program was a supervised exercise program tailored to my needs.

My husband had been transporting me to the center since April 2012 for my fitness program Monday, Wednesday, and Friday from seven-forty-five a.m. to eight-forty-five a.m. However, as I exited the building on September twenty-fourth, I was instructed by the voice of the Holy Spirit, "Drive home." I walked to the car where my husband was in the driver's seat, and I said, "The Holy Spirit told me to drive home." Wilbert just moved to the passenger side without any discussion. Without any fear, I drove on the interstate to home. I literally did not concentrate on the daily nerve pain that I usually have in my right thumb and in my upper right arm. Throughout the week of September twenty-fourth, 2012, I was encouraged to drive to pre-scheduled doctors appointments, to the grocery store, and to other necessary places.

When the Holy Spirit spoke to me, my first response was to trust and obey, since I had not driven since August 2010. I immediately responded to the Holy Spirit. We are to submit to God, for what He says is for our own good. We bring him honor, and we bring ourselves blessings, by doing His will. It begins with listening. The Holy Spirit presented a choice for action. It did not demand or force. It was a still, small, strong thought or impression in my spirit. Each of us must listen in the way that He chooses to deal with us. The important thing is that we listen—that we are ready and willing to hear what He says. We should be looking for His leadership rather than ignoring it.

The Holy Spirit isn't involved in idle words. He does not call attention to himself and is often silent because He has already given you enough information and advice (John 15:26 NKJV). He wants you to use what He has already given; He has been training your conscience to respond rightly to what faces you. That does not mean that you rely on yourself, but that you rely on what God has already done in your life and what He has already taught you.

The Holy Spirit is God at work in our lives. Everything God does is done through His Spirit. Paul, therefore, encourages us in Ephesians 4:30 (NKJV), "And do not grieve the Holy Spirit of God...." Be attentive to what the Spirit says. When He speaks, God is speaking.

The Amazing Grace of God

When we speak of God's grace, we mean all the good gifts we enjoy in life. The gift of life includes the wondrous gift of being human.

During my sickness, my focus was on how great our God is. My heart, mind, and soul focused on the Giver of life and not to rely on my own strength, but on God's amazing grace. The expression, "the grace of God" prompts pleasant and peaceful thoughts about our Father, the Great Creator.

What is grace?

When Paul used the phrase "the grace of God" in Titus 2:11, it was for a specific purpose. The expression refers to the Savior of mankind, which is Jesus. He is the gift of God's grace by which all men may be saved. He saved us, not because of deeds done by us in righteousness, but in virtue of His own mercy "through the washing of regeneration and renewing of the Holy Spirit, whom He poured out on us abundantly through Jesus Christ our Savior"

(Titus 3: 4-6 NKJV). Jesus experienced death so that every man who dies needs not stay dead forever.

I have been changed by grace, shaped by grace, strengthened by grace, emboldened by grace, and softened by grace. I experienced that grace comes after you. It revives you from insecure to God secure. Grace is the voice that calls us to change and then gives us the power to pull it off.

On the other side of the coin, the pain in my right thumb, wrist, and the upper part of my right arm has accrued a thousand needles, making a nest in those areas. In spite of the pain, God's grace allows me to use my right hand to write and to use the computer. Sometimes God takes us through stages in order for us to complete His maturing process. I'm a living witness that God's amazing grace kills the pain better than Tylenol or any other painkiller. If there are no trials, there can be no growing in grace, no equipping for special blessings. Under the spell of God's beauty, there is nothing to fear. God will paint bright colors on the canvass of your life if you stay steadfast in your faith.

God walked with me when the journey was difficult to travel. God's presence guided me through the high peaks of my sickness. He heard my cries of thanksgiving and joy. God was my guide. He quenched my thirst for knowledge and filled my days with challenges. That is the amazing grace of God.

In spite of all my sufferings and what I have been through, I'm a walking, talking, living, breathing miracle of God's grace. He is keeping me around for a reason. Whatever it is, I will pour my life into it.

Like Job, I will trust in the Lord and look forward to my reward. I will stand firm without fear, for God is "my light and my salvation; whom shall I fear? . . ." (Psalm 27:1). I'm so grateful that God has given me the ability to walk again and to be useful at home. Being able to do certain household chores and to cook complete meals is a step up for me.

Now I have a chance and the faith to launch out into the deep to tell the world what God has done for me. I thank God for allowing me to try something beyond what I have already mastered so that I can continue to grow. Jesus said, "According to your faith let it be to you" (Matthew 9:29 (NKJV)).

I have improved a great deal, however, I have learned not to dwell on my aches and pains because everybody has troubles. People in the hospital would gladly trade places with me. With God's grace, I can prevail over my circumstances. I can rise above discouragement and the self-defeating mentality that says, "Nothing is going to change for the better." In my spirit, I knew that God was moving me from one degree of grace to another; therefore, I labored and cooperated with it for my own spiritual development.

God's grace is so amazing because His grace is free and because we do not deserve it. We are given grace to repent, grace to believe, grace to be saved. We are given grace to understand the Word of God. We are given grace to defeat temptation. We are given grace to endure suffering, disappointment, and pain. We are given grace to obey the Lord. We are given grace to serve Him by using our spiritual gifts, which are gifts of grace. This great grace is received through obedient faith.

God's Grace Is Sufficient

When I reviewed 2 Corinthians 12:9, ". . . My grace is sufficient for thee: for my strength is made perfect in weakness," it made me take another look at myself. By searching this scripture, I found out that grace enables you to make it no matter what. No matter who turns against you, no matter what obstacles you face, no matter how many times you fail, God's incredible grace is there to pick you up, to revive lost hope, to heal broken bones, and to strengthen your weak will. It is never incapable, nor is it ever exhausted. There is no timeline attached because it will never decay or run out.

Throughout my journey, I wanted to make God's grace a reality in my life. I asked God, how do I do this? I learned that I simply had to claim the promises in His Word. I had to tell Him my need and abandon my own efforts and trust Him to work things out for me. I had to be sensitive to see and hear the leading of His Spirit.

His grace guided and directed me when I wanted to give up. His grace heard my cry and carried my burdens and sorrows of sickness.

I prayed that the pain in my right wrist, thumb, and arm be removed; however, my request has been delayed. God is letting me know that He has given me His grace, and that is enough. Paul said in 2 Corinthians 12:7-9 (NKJV), "... a thorn in the flesh was given to me, a messenger of Satan to buffet me, lest I be exalted above measure. Concerning this thing I pleaded with the Lord three times that it might depart from me. And He said to me, 'My grace is sufficient for you, for My strength is made perfect in weakness.'" We can learn from Paul that there are times when God, having given us His grace, hears our appeals and says, "My grace is sufficient for you."

Some say the thorn in St. Paul's flesh was the fact that his eyesight was defective. For when he fell under the convincing power of God, he was blind for three days and nights, and his eyesight was never entirely restored. That was the thorn in his flesh. Others have said that the thorn in Paul's flesh was a defect in one of his legs because he had a limp as he went through the world, carrying the Gospel. Many believed that the thorn in St. Paul's flesh was the continued suppression of the ambition of his nature. Paul was eminently a great man.

We may ask ourselves, "What is my thorn?" There is not a person without a thorn. Paul did not tell what his thorn was. St. Paul carried this thorn in his flesh, the messenger of Satan to buffet him. He carried it until he felt in his heart, "I can carry it no longer." Many of us struggle with this problem because it is too much to bear. Like Paul, we have to fall on our knees and pray to God for help and mercy. Paul prayed earnestly, but the thorn was still in his flesh, with all of its unspeakable pain. Paul looked for help from his friends, but they turned their backs on him. The third time Paul prayed, he reflected on the blessed Christ as He prayed in the Garden of Gethsemane. God reached down and put His hand on the thorn in Paul's flesh and drove it up and said, "My grace is sufficient for thee..." (2 Corinthians 12:9).

When we go to God, and He puts His hand on that thorn and drives it up and says, "My grace is sufficient for thee..." (2 Corinthians 12:9), trust Him and He will give us strength. When we are weak, we are going to be strengthened under Him.

When we have weak moments in our lives, God shows His power and love. May God help us to trust Him and help us to see that whatever our thorn is, He will take care of it for us. We wonder why God doesn't remove certain things in our life. If He did, we might depend on our own strength instead of God's grace. God wants us to accept His free gift of grace so we will live a life for Him in a way to serve Him. All of life is a gift of grace. We must learn to live a gracious life of forgiving others and loving others. Learning how to be a disciple of Christ makes us use the faith that we have.

God's grace is sufficient to survive pains—physical, spiritual, or emotional. God's grace is sufficient for everything. When God's grace is sufficient, it is more than enough. I went through a process of learning to own or accept the trial I was experiencing due to my illness. God was leading me to glorify Him through my illness. The Holy Sprit led me to reflect back to November twenty-third, 1960 when I gave birth to my second child, Andrea. After her birth, I sought employment as a teacher because a job was not guaranteed when you went out on maternity leave. In an effort to seek a teaching position, I went for an interview at the central office on a snow blizzard day, which was classified as the coldest day of the year. No good news came out of this effort, but God had a ram in the bush. A member of my home church, who was a principal, recommended me to teach second grade at her school.

When sickness struck in June 2010, an x-ray showed arthritis on my spine. I reflected back to 1961 when my body was exposed to a blizzard. God's grace allowed me to expect a healing and to demand a dependence on Him.

I went through seasons and storms, but God's grace gave me visibility to see through the darkness. As I struggled in my weaknesses, the Holy Spirit sanctioned me to boast about God's power and glory. My weaknesses were designed by God for the purpose of humbling me and glorifying Jesus, His Son. My struggle with sickness intensified the love of Jesus because He rolled back the curtain of death to give me life.

The Power of God's Presence

Adrian Rogers in his article titled "The Glory of God's Presence" suggests that God is so powerful because He is omnipresent, which means that He is everywhere, not just at church. He sees everything and knows everything about us. We can find glory in God's presence when we spend time in prayer with Him, just to be alone with Him to share our fears as well as our joys.[6]

I was reminded that prayer is a privilege and a way to build up a strong relationship with God. One can feel God's presence when we worship Him in holiness and learn to seek God through the trials of life. Thank God I learned during my recovery to put God first in my daily living and practice His presence.

In the midst of my suffering and pain, I felt God's presence and found hope. God did not let me lose hope in Him in spite of the pains. He gave me comfort in spite of everything. I had faith that I could accomplish anything with God's presence. I thank God for my husband who had faith in me when he was asked by the Pastor to assume the leadership of a special program in the church. He replied, "Yes, if my wife can work along with me." The presence of God dispels darkness and brings life. When we experience storms in our lives, such as suffering, bereavement, discouragement, danger, and difficulty, we need comfort from God's presence in the darkness of these storms. When we call out to God as we pass through dark valleys, believe and have faith in His sovereignty. We are not ruled by chance but by a God who is in control and exists when we call on Him.

Storms of life are impartial. They happen to good people, they happen to bad people. They happen to believers, they happen to unbelievers. They happen to all. Matthew 5:45 (NKJV) says, "that you may be sons of your Father in heaven; for He makes His sun rise on the evil and on the good, and sends rain on the just and on the unjust." Being a Christian does not exempt us from being in storms.

The disciples got into a storm because they obeyed God. Jesus told them to get in the boat. They got in the boat, and they sailed right into a storm.

> After he had dismissed them, he went up on a mountainside by himself to pray. When evening came, he was there alone, but the boat was already a considerable distance from the land, buffeted by

the waves because the wind was against it. During the fourth watch of the night, Jesus went out to them, walking on the lake. When the disciples saw him walking on the lake, they were terrified. "It's a ghost," they said, and cried out in fear. But Jesus immediately said to them: "Take courage! It is I. Don't be afraid." "Lord, if it's you," Peter replied, "tell me to come to you on the water." "Come," he said. Then Peter got down out of the boat, walked on the water and came toward Jesus. But when he saw the wind, he was afraid and, beginning to sink, cried out, "Lord, save me!" Immediately Jesus reached out his hand and caught him. "You of little faith," he said, "why did you doubt?" And when they climbed into the boat, the wind died down. Then those who were in the boat worshiped him, saying, "Truly you are the Son of God." (Matthew 14:22-33 NIV)

Do we call on our Heavenly Father and His Son when the waters of anguish began to fill our ship? Or do we have the faith to trust Christ?

We must remember there is someone who can bring peace when we are being tossed so hard that we feel like we can barely hang on. Sometimes in life, we just try to outlast the storm, forgetting to call on the One who can calm it. Peace may not come when we want it. Peace may not come the way we want it. When we call on the Master and allow Him to bear our burdens, our peace may come in small reminders of His love and care, giving us strength to get through the storm.

When you are going through a rough time, don't automatically assume, "I must be out of the will of God." You may be exactly where God wants you to be. God has not promised us a storm free life. Many times, Christians endure unhappiness when they go their way and never have taken time to get to know God. When we take time to get to know God, we trust Him in our lives.

When your boat is rocking, trust God. Experiencing God's presence is not an accident, but a blessing. When you yearn for peace and comfort, He is there. When you pray for a good night's sleep, He is there. At times, God's presence was exciting for me when I walked alone, leaning on His strength. Many times, I found the courage to walk at a brisk pace, leaving my accompanying friends or family.

The presence of God is not only a physical manifestation, but also an undeniable knowledge that He is with you. When you abide in Him in deep intimacy and complete surrender, His presence is overwhelming. The Holy Spirit made residence in my life when I allowed God's presence to manifest itself in my life.

Man's Promise Keeper

We all make and break promises for many reasons. Sometimes we forget what we promise, or it may be due to circumstances beyond our control. Nevertheless, a promise not kept by man can break our heart. On the other side of the coin—the promises made by God to man—we can stand on these promises for God is a faithful Promise Keeper.

The American Heritage Dictionary gives the following as a definition of promise. Promise: A declaration assuring that one will or will not do something; vow.[7]

Middletown Bible Church's Bible study on Spiritual Life expresses God's promises:

> Many of God's promises are conditional (when you see the word "conditional" just think of the little word "if"). God promises to do something, **IF** man does something. God will do His part **if** man does his part.

When God gives an unconditional promise, there are no "if's", "and's", or " but's" about it! God says," I WILL DO SOMETHING" and it does not matter if men like it, or don't like it, believe it or don't believe it— God is still going to do it! An unconditional promise means that GOD WILL do what He promised no matter what![8]

We must believe God's promises by faith. It is an investment that penetrates a blazing light to dim all fear and doubt.

I thank God for the promises He has made for us as Christians through His Word: freedom from the penalty of sin, eternal life with Him, His abiding presence and peace for our hearts. On the other side of the coin, we should never make the mistake of confusing God's promises with our own high expectations. God has not promised that we would never be hungry. He has not promised that we will have the kind of life that seems desirable. He has not promised that we will have the family that we want. There are many things in this life that can dash our hopes, but God's promises are sure. We can retain our faith in Him because we know He will always be faithful to us.

Since my operation on my spine in the neck area, I have improved tremendously because God's presence in my life has increased my faith 100%. I have had time to grow through my difficult times by focusing on God's strength and praising Him for my progress thus far. My persistent prayer life helps me to hold on and not to give up. The Bible says, "But they that wait upon the Lord shall renew their strength; they shall mount up with wings as eagles; they shall run, and not be weary; they shall walk and not faint" (Isaiah 40:31).

In spite of any pain I encountered, I refused to fret or worry, but trusted God's timetable for a complete healing. I accepted the delays because God has promised that His grace is sufficient for us. It is through an obedient faith that we have access into the grace of God according to Romans 5:2.

I shall never forget what God has done in my life as I wait on His promises of healing. We tend to forget God's power. We tend to forget how important it is to stay in God's strength and to stop focusing on all of our problems than on what He has done for us.

I thank God for being my Promise Keeper on my journey. Everything I did was based upon faith in the promises of God. God has promised that all things work together for good for those who love and serve Him faithfully (Romans 8:28). It may be difficult for us to see and understand how this is accomplished at times, but God has promised it, and He will deliver.

Let me appeal to the readers of my journey to live so that the promises of God will be yours.

When Fear Knocks

Fear is an emotion. Many people live by fear. They live in fear of sickness. They live in fear of germs. They live in fear of speaking in front of a group. They live in fear of losing their jobs. They live in fear of losing their spouses. They live in fear of spiders, animals, bad weather. They hold on to the fear of "What If?" None of these are present or potent. It is being afraid of something that may or may not happen. You can conquer your fears by understanding why you are afraid. If something is present and potent, there is cause to be afraid. That is the emotion that you are supposed to feel. If you are in an earthquake, then it is present and potent and you should feel afraid. But if you are thinking of an earthquake and it is not present and potent, then you should not be afraid.[9]

When fear knocks, what should you do? Christians should handle fear by trusting God when they are afraid or doubt life. The Bible says in Proverbs 3:5, "Trust in the Lord with all thine heart; and lean not unto thine own understanding." You must lean on God's understanding because His love casts out all fear. You can bring peace to your life by trusting in the Lord. [10] Trusting releases control to God. As you release more and more of your fears to Him, you demonstrate "in short: more God, less you!"[11] This can really be developed into a formula for your life: to trust God more equals more peace in your life.

When fear knocks, know that the Lord "... is always there on the inside, no matter what's happening outside. . . . He will keep you [us] safe in your [our] heart [hearts]."[12] Always focus on God to get you through life and hard times. Don't stay up all night worrying about your problems. God never sleeps or slumbers. He will take care of your problems.

On my journey, I was challenged with thoughts such as, "Will I be able to walk again, be independent, and be able to take care of basic needs?" In spite of knowing that God promised in His Word that He would take care of me, Satan attempted to challenge God's promises with fear. The choice was mine. Would I listen and believe the Word of God or the lies of Satan?

Thank God, when fear knocked in my life, I put my fear under the blood of Jesus so it would be washed away forever. I refused to let my fears grow and be entertained with threats of the future. Jesus paid it all. His blood paid for the fears I was battling.

Remember, when fear knocks, don't answer. Overcome fear with power, love, and a sound mind.

When Worry Wages

Worry can't change our past or future, but it can ruin the present. When we dwell in the past or future, we lack motivation to make progress now. Therefore, we should not waste time worrying; instead, cast your burden on the Lord. When worry wages, put your trust in the Lord and believe in His Sovereign power and His will. Be patient and live on the Lord's agenda rather than your own ideas. Our hearts should be filled with God's love and hope; our minds are to be grounded in God's truth.[13]

God's people are not exempted from the troubles of this life. We can endure whatever hardships come our way without being defeated when we stand strong in the love, hope, and truth that God provides. Therefore, don't worry about anything; instead, pray about everything. Worry cannot add to your life. Therefore, abolish worry and substitute God's power and strength to demolish the weeds in your life.

Matthew 6:34 (NIV) says, "Therefore do not worry about tomorrow, for tomorrow will worry about itself. Each day has enough trouble of its own."

After my surgery, I remained in intensive care for two days. During that time, I was in another world. I could hear the movement of furniture and lots of discussion in the background. I yelled out, "Wilbert, call Andrea and tell her to make plans for my funeral." I could hear him say, "You are not dead." Before the sedation for the surgery, the prayers that my family rendered were embedded in my spirit, reminding me that God was with me. There was peace and security in reflecting whether my life would be extended in this world or with my God and Jesus Christ, my Savior.

What kept me moving in a positive direction during my recovery from illness was that I realized that I had no power of my own. Therefore, I prayed to the Lord daily for His strength. I quickly realized that I needed the Lord's strength to meet my daily challenges. Psalm 37:4 (NKJV) says, "Delight yourself also in the Lord, And He shall give you the desires of your heart." Isaiah 40:31 (NKJV) says, "But those who wait on the Lord shall renew their strength; They shall mount up with wings like eagles, They shall run and not be weary, They shall walk and not faint."

As you journey through life, enjoy the scenery as you mope along the path you are taking. Never let anxiety and impatience direct your speed or take you to another route. Let the Divine Providence steer you toward a brighter view.

When you became a Christian, you began a journey that will last the rest of your life. For most people, this journey is many years long. You reach your destination when you pass through the gate of death into eternal life.

Jesus, the Pioneer of our salvation, made this journey ahead of us. He blazed the trail and broke down all barriers. The way, however, is still long and difficult. Many who start do not reach the end. Only those who keep their eyes fixed on Jesus and faithfully follow in His footsteps reach the goal.

When Life Is Broken

My faith journey allowed me the opportunity to recognize the restoration power of God as I recovered from my sickness. Satan tried to kill my hope, joy, and faith in God. He tried to take away my dreams and my health. Whatever hardships I encountered during my illness, God put me back on track. My brokenness was repaired, however. Sometimes we think that life is beyond repair when everything looks dark and hopeless. The journey that I took with God on faith was not hopeless. No matter how dark life looks, with Christ, our future is bright. God is a God of new things. A new life, a new beginning, a new covenant, a new heart, and a new way of doing things. Because He is a God of new things, there is always hope and a future. There is joy and peace. The Scripture says, "But I will restore you to health and heal your wounds,' declares the Lord" (Jeremiah 30:17 NIV).

I struggled with a lot of questions about my recovery from pain due to my illness. But now I know how to jump over hurdles.

On my faith journey, I learned to open up my heart for God's healing and leaned on the master craftsman. He specializes in taking what is not and creating what is. He is in the business of restoring hopes, broken dreams, wounded spirits, and hopeless lives. He beckons us to bring to Him our situation that seems hopeless, dim, broken, beyond repair, and without luster. God can restore and make it new. There is nothing beyond His power of restoration, for God can restore, can forgive, and can take a broken vessel and remake and refashion it all over again.

When God put my body back together again, many people responded, "You don't look like you've ever been sick."

People in restaurants and public places that I did not know offered compliments on a regular basis about my physical look, dress attire, and over-all appearance. My image was on display, and my eyes glistered with joy. These expressions and comments forced me to blush and feel young at heart. However, the embodiment of grace and strength cradled in my heart to personify protection. I was on exhibit with my heartbeat throbbing, saying a silent prayer, "God, thank you for making my day a blessing to my soul and for putting me back together again. Your grace is sufficient."

You don't have to try to fix the problem on your own and be weighed down by the cares of this world. Let it go and let God take care of it. Don't try to clean up by yourself. Jesus will give you peace and hope. Allow Him to restore you lovingly, and you will never be the same again. When you bring your brokenness to Him and ask Him to restore you, He will set you free from the things in your past. When God restores your life, He will make it a brand new life. He will give you a resurrection and will restore what you have lost. If you have "done things that are [your] own fault, or whether it is the enemy who has stolen from [you], God is still the Restorer!"[14]

Jesus practiced the principle of restoration. In Acts 10:38, we find, "How God anointed Jesus of Nazareth with the Holy Ghost and with power: who went about doing good, and healing all that were oppressed of the devil; for God was with Him."

In Mark 8:25, Jesus practiced the principle of restoration when He put His hands on the blind man's eyes "and made him look up: and he was restored and saw every man clearly."

In Matthew 12:13 (NKJV), Jesus told the man with a withered hand to stretch out his hand "and he stretched it out, and it was restored as whole as the other."

Restoration is realized by your faith in God and His Word and your declaration of that truth. I thank God for delivering up His own Son for us all so He can deliver us and restore us when we call out for help.

Lessons Learned On My Journey

On my journey, God's grace enabled me to understand that my journey would not delete trials and tribulations. However, I endured my trials because I learned to spend proper time with the Word and develop a personal relationship with God. Being human, sometimes we talk to people about our trials. However, don't tell your troubles to the wrong people. Look for people who will share your burdens, not spread your problems. Take your troubles to the Lord and leave them there. I learned that when you approach the throne of grace with confidence, you will receive mercy and find grace to help you in times of need.

My journey strengthened my faithfulness to God. When we are walking in faith, God intends for us to develop our faith. God made a way of escape for me in order for me to be able to bear my pains and discomfort. The testing grounds that I went through let me know that I had to endure patience. God had a solution for my problem in spite of the times I felt down and level to the ground. I realized that Satan's strategy was to defeat me by wearing me down. However, I knew that I would be a winner because of God's love for me. For every problem, God has a solution. Winning is not a matter of escape, but endurance.

Conclusion

Faith should be a life-changing encounter with Christ. Often, we go through a test of faith, whether it's a dilemma in our personal lives, our health and well being, or in our relationships. Yet, there are also those rare moments when we realize that in the midst of a personal crisis, the answers come unexpectedly. It is in those rare moments that we must realize that we have had a life-changing encounter in faith. Jesus does not eliminate all the suffering and storms from your life, but He can give you strength and a supernatural peace even in the midst of the storms.

Faith goes deeper than feelings—we are to walk with Christ by faith, even when our feelings may be negative or neutral. Our commitment of faith and love for Christ needs to go far beyond our feelings. If we only walked with Christ when we felt good, we would be serving Christ out of our own selfishness. Love is tested, and love grows by staying faithful through the challenging times.

In dark times of seeming defeat, always remember that behind every circumstance, there is a supernatural power at work—the King, our Lord and Savior, Jesus Christ. Allow the King to move in your life to achieve your destiny.

No matter how desperate your situation—it may even look like you have lost everything—keep the faith because the King, our Lord and Savior, Jesus Christ, promised in Matthew 17:20 that ". . . nothing shall be impossible unto you."

End Notes

1. Marijohn Wilkin and Kris Kristofferson, "One Day At A Time." (Nashville, TN: Buckhorn Music Publishing, 1974), 4.

2. Smith Wigglesworth, Smith Wigglesworth on Faith (New Kensington, PA: Whitaker House, 1998), 44.

3. Ibid., 125.

4. Jack Zavada, "Book of Job: Introduction to the Book of Job", About.com, Bible Study Tools Old Testament Books of The Bible, http://christianity.about.com/od/oldtestamentbooks/a/JZ-Book-Of-Job.htm (last accessed June 14, 2014).

5. Ibid.

6. Adrian Rogers, "The Glory of God's Presence", Thursday, July 16, 2009, LoveWorthFinding Ministries with Adrian Rogers, http://www.lwf.org/site/News2?abbr=for_&page=NewsArticle&id=9725&news_iv_ctrl=1261 (last accessed December 3, 2013).

7. American Heritage Dictionary, Second College ed., s.v. "promise."

8. Middletown Bible Church, "Chapter 9 Believing God's Promises," Spiritual Life lesson, http://www.middletownbiblechurch.org/spiritua/spirit9.htm (last accessed April 4, 2014).

9. Shane Ede, "Overcoming Fear", Posted January 3, 2011, 21st Century Human (On The Journey To A 21st Century Renaissance), http://www.21stcenturyhuman.com/articles/overcoming-fear/ (last accessed June 13, 2014).

10. Rev. Ethan McCardell, "Seeking Answers—Life is Full of Questions", Question 1, Dealing with Fear and Worry, 2009 Issue 5, ISSN 2163-7768 (Online), The New Church (New Church Connection), http://www.newchurch.org/connection/issues/dealing-with-fear-and-worry/life-is-full-of-questions.html (last accessed April 30, 2014).

11. Ibid., Question 4.

12. Ibid.

13. Mary Fairchild, "4 Reasons Not to Worry", About.com, Topical Devotions, http://christianity.about.com/od/whatdoesthebiblesay/qt/reasonnot2worry.htm (last accessed December 3, 2013).

14. Brenda Thomas, "The Restoration Power of God", The Kenneth Hagin Ministries Study Center Articles, Kenneth Hagin Ministries, http://www.rhema.org/index.php?option=com_content&view=article&id=1077:the-restoration-power-of-god&Itemid=304 (last accessed November 19, 2012).

CPSIA information can be obtained at www.ICGtesting.com
Printed in the USA
BVOW05s1940170315

392111BV00001B/2/P

9 781498 427791